Preface and Notes on Structure

This document describes the Generative Deve
(GDF) in detail. GDF is presented as a **stand-alone framework**. It includes:

- **Phases and Progressions**: An overview of the lifecycle GDF envisions for generative AI-driven software initiatives.
- **Knowledge Areas**: Each knowledge area addresses specific challenges, inputs, and outputs relevant to implementing and scaling generative development.
- **Roles and Responsibilities**: Spanning from portfolio-level stakeholders to development teams, compliance officers, and customer-facing roles.
- **Artifacts and Documentation**: Inputs and outputs that guide execution and help standardize the use of generative AI.

PART I: INTRODUCTION & FRAMEWORK OVERVIEW

Chapter 1: Purpose of GDF

1.1 Why GDF?

Modern enterprises face the challenge of rapidly evolving technologies alongside mounting pressure to **reduce time-to-market** and **increase software quality**. Generative AI—especially large language models (LLMs)—presents new opportunities to automate code generation, testing, documentation, and design tasks. The **Generative Development Framework (GDF)** helps organizations **formalize** the integration of these technologies into their software engineering processes.

- **Efficiency Gains**: Automate repetitive coding tasks to free developers for higher-value work.
- **Quality Improvements**: Enforce best practices and coding standards through well-crafted AI prompts and verification processes.
- **Scalability**: Provide a roadmap for teams to expand from small AI pilots to enterprise-wide programs.

1.2 Distinguishing Features

1. **Phased Progression**: Each project follows a lifecycle that accommodates iterative updates and feedback from generative models.
2. **Knowledge Areas**: GDF identifies 18 distinct domains of practice, from Ideation to Scaling & Sustaining.
3. **Integrated View of People, Processes, and Technology**: Emphasizes organizational readiness, stakeholder involvement, and compliance considerations, in parallel with technical workflows.

Chapter 2: GDF Phases and Process Flow

GDF organizes generative development initiatives into **six major phases,** each with defined inputs, outputs, activities, and artifacts. These phases are intended to be **iterative** and **adaptive**, allowing teams to cycle back if needed.

1. **Phase 1: Strategy & Preparation**
   - **Inputs**: Corporate strategy documents, portfolio objectives, technical feasibility assessments.
   - **Activities**: Identify and prioritize potential AI use cases. Assess readiness in terms of data availability, tools, and skills. Secure executive sponsorship.
   - **Outputs**: High-level project charter (or equivalent), readiness checklist, stakeholder matrix.
2. **Phase 2: Scoping & Planning**

- o **Inputs**: Project charter, domain requirements, high-level architecture or design standards.
- o **Activities**: Define scope boundaries, outline generative tasks (e.g., code generation, test generation), set success metrics, create a resource plan (human and computational).
- o **Outputs**: Detailed generative AI plan, communication approach, risk register, architecture blueprint.

3. **Phase 3: Generation & Iteration**
   - o **Inputs**: Detailed requirements, prompts or prompt templates, dataset for training/fine-tuning.
   - o **Activities**: Develop or refine AI models (if needed), generate code or other artifacts, iterate based on feedback. Integrate generative outputs into existing development pipelines.
   - o **Outputs**: AI-generated artifacts (code modules, documentation, UI components), updated prompt libraries, iteration logs.

4. **Phase 4: Validation & Integration**
   - o **Inputs**: Generated artifacts, acceptance criteria, testing frameworks, security and compliance standards.
   - o **Activities**: Validate artifacts via automated tests, peer reviews, or specialized QA steps. Integrate approved artifacts into the broader system, ensuring alignment with security and regulatory standards.
   - o **Outputs**: Verified codebase, compliance check results, integrated systems or microservices, QA documentation.

5. **Phase 5: Deployment & Monitoring**
   - o **Inputs**: Verified software, deployment runbooks, monitoring/observability tools.
   - o **Activities**: Deploy generative solutions to staging or production environments, configure monitoring for performance and drift in AI-generated components. Gather usage data and user feedback.
   - o **Outputs**: Production deployments, usage metrics, stakeholder feedback reports, updated maintenance backlog.

6. **Phase 6: Sustainment & Evolution**
   - ○ **Inputs**: Production metrics, end-user feedback, change requests, updated organizational strategy.
   - ○ **Activities**: Continuously refine AI models or prompts, plan future improvements or expansions, address any technical debt. Celebrate milestones and success stories to reinforce adoption.
   - ○ **Outputs**: Updated model versions, improved development processes, post-implementation review, new or extended use-case proposals.

Chapter 3: Roles and Responsibilities

3.1 Portfolio-Level Stakeholders

- **Executive Sponsor**: Champions generative AI at the leadership level, secures funding, and aligns projects with strategic goals.
- **Portfolio Manager**: Prioritizes initiatives across multiple AI projects, ensuring resource allocation aligns with ROI and corporate needs.

3.2 Product-Level Stakeholders

- **Product Owner**: Defines functional requirements, sets priorities, and manages the backlog for generative AI features or tasks.
- **Business Analyst**: Gathers and refines requirements, translating them into clear prompts or specifications for generative tasks.

3.3 Development Teams

- **Generative AI Engineer**: Crafts prompts, fine-tunes models, and sets up pipelines to integrate AI outputs with existing codebases.

- **Software Developer**: Collaborates with AI-generated code, provides domain expertise for iteration and debugging, and ensures final code meets acceptance criteria.
- **QA Engineer/Tester**: Validates AI-generated solutions via automated tests, code reviews, or user acceptance testing.

3.4 Regulatory, Security, and Compliance

- **Compliance Officer**: Ensures adherence to data privacy, regulatory requirements, and internal policies across generative workflows.
- **Security Specialist**: Conducts vulnerability assessments on AI-generated code, ensuring secrets, sensitive data, and access controls are handled properly.

3.5 Customer and End-User Roles

- **User Representative or Customer Liaison**: Provides real-world feedback on user experience, helps refine acceptance criteria, and signals additional needs or areas for improvement.

Chapter 4: GDF Knowledge Areas Overview

GDF comprises **18 Knowledge Areas**, each aligned with a distinct facet of generative AI adoption. These areas cut across the six phases and serve as **"lenses"** through which the project activities should be viewed.

1. **Ideation**
2. **Specification**
3. **Generation**
4. **Transformation**
5. **Replacement**
6. **Integration**
7. **Separation**
8. **Consolidation**

9. **Templating**
10. **Visualization**
11. **Verification**
12. **Implementation**
13. **Optimization**
14. **Security & Risk Management**
15. **Generative Pipelines**
16. **Compliance & Governance**
17. **Collaboration & Communication**
18. **Scaling & Sustaining**

4.1 Knowledge Area Inputs, Outputs, and Artifacts

Each Knowledge Area includes:

- **Inputs**: Information, resources, or tools needed (e.g., dataset, code standards, user stories).
- **Outputs**: Tangible or intangible results, like a code module, a compliance checklist, or a stakeholder alignment map.
- **Artifacts**: Documented templates, design schematics, user manuals, or code generation logs that record the progression and decisions made.

Chapter 5: Example Use Case

5.1 Overview of a Hypothetical Enterprise Project

Scenario: A large retail enterprise wants to introduce an AI-assisted tool that automatically generates new microservices for its inventory management system.

1. **Phase 1 – Strategy & Preparation**
   - **Inputs**: Corporate strategy emphasizing supply chain modernization. Data from existing inventory systems.
   - **Activities**: Identify the microservice use case (e.g., reorder request generation). Assess data readiness and internal skill sets.

- **Outputs**: High-level blueprint outlining required features, sponsor sign-off, generative AI readiness checklist.
2. **Phase 2 – Scoping & Planning**
   - **Inputs**: High-level blueprint, stakeholder input.
   - **Activities**: Define the scope of the generative tasks, such as code snippet generation or automated test generation for each microservice function. Develop a risk register considering data privacy in the supply chain.
   - **Outputs**: Detailed plan with timeline, resource assignment, compliance guidelines.
3. **Phase 3 – Generation & Iteration**
   - **Inputs**: Fine-tuned LLM on corporate coding standards, domain data for inventory logic.
   - **Activities**: Generate code stubs for new microservices (e.g., purchase order creation). Developers integrate stubs into the environment, providing iterative feedback to refine prompts and model outputs.
   - **Outputs**: Code stubs, prompt library updates, integration logs documenting any code modifications.
4. **Phase 4 – Validation & Integration**
   - **Inputs**: Generated code, test frameworks, QA guidelines.
   - **Activities**: Conduct functional tests and security audits on AI-generated services, integrate validated microservices into the overall architecture, update configuration management repositories.
   - **Outputs**: Certified and integrated microservices, test results, compliance sign-off.
5. **Phase 5 – Deployment & Monitoring**
   - **Inputs**: Validated microservices, deployment runbook.
   - **Activities**: Deploy new services to the production cluster, monitor performance for anomalies or drift from expected logic. Gather real-time analytics on usage and developer feedback.
   - **Outputs**: Production-ready microservices, usage dashboards, performance and drift metrics.
6. **Phase 6 – Sustainment & Evolution**

- Inputs: Performance metrics, user feedback, new potential features from the backlog.
- Activities: Retrain or fine-tune AI models for new requirements or improved performance. Plan next wave of microservices or expansions to other domains (e.g., shipping, warehousing).
- Outputs: Updated generative AI roadmap, new backlog items, lessons learned integrated into the broader enterprise AI strategy.

PART II: GDF KNOWLEDGE AREAS IN DEPTH

In this section, we explore each **Knowledge Area** of the Generative Development Framework (GDF) in detail. We discuss their definitions, typical inputs and outputs, key artifacts, and real-world examples to illustrate best practices.

Note: Originally, GDF enumerated 18 Knowledge Areas (having removed an ethics-specific domain). This edition introduces a new, separate Knowledge Area on **Competency** (Knowledge Area #19) to address the vital role of human expertise in generative AI projects.

Chapter 6: Ideation

Definition
Ideation focuses on discovering opportunities where generative AI can meaningfully enhance or automate the software development lifecycle. It includes brainstorming sessions, user research, and feasibility studies to outline initial ideas.

Inputs

- **Business Objectives**: Documents or strategic goals that indicate where improvements or innovation are needed.

- **Technical Feasibility Assessments**: Preliminary evaluations of data availability, model readiness, and infrastructure.
- **Stakeholder Feedback**: Insights from product owners, developers, operations teams, and customers on pain points.

Outputs

- **Proposed Use Cases**: A collection of potential areas where generative AI can add value (e.g., code generation, test automation).
- **Prioritized Idea List**: A ranked set of initiatives, usually based on ROI or strategic alignment.

Artifacts

- **Idea Sheets**: Simple one-page documents summarizing each generative AI concept.
- **Feasibility Checklists**: Templates ensuring each idea is viable regarding technology, cost, and organizational readiness.

Example

A large financial institution gathers top developers and product leads to brainstorm how AI might reduce time spent on boilerplate code for internal services. They produce **Idea Sheets** detailing multiple possibilities, eventually prioritizing a pilot project focused on automated documentation generation.

Chapter 7: Specification

Definition
Specification translates the high-level concepts from Ideation into concrete requirements for AI-driven development tasks. It details desired outputs (e.g., code quality standards, UI design frameworks), acceptance criteria, and integration points.

Inputs

- **User Stories / Requirements**: Detailed functional and non-functional needs.
- **Technical Constraints**: Preferred programming languages, frameworks, or data schema definitions.
- **Regulatory Requirements**: Compliance obligations that the AI outputs must satisfy (e.g., data-handling mandates).

Outputs

- **Generative Requirements**: A specification of what the AI model or prompt should produce (code, documentation, UI assets) and how it should be validated.
- **Technical Architecture Outline**: A basic layout or blueprint describing how generative outputs will fit into the existing system.

Artifacts

- **Prompt Templates**: Structured prompt examples that developers can reuse and modify.
- **Design Diagrams**: High-level architecture charts or UI mockups aligning with generative tasks.

Example

In a logistics application, the **Specification** phase defines a prompt template:

"Generate a RESTful Node.js service called ShipmentTracker that connects to an existing MySQL database and returns shipment status in JSON format. The code should be TypeScript, include basic error handling, and must adhere to corporate coding standards."

Chapter 8: Generation

Definition
Generation is where actual outputs—such as code stubs, documentation, or test scenarios—are produced by AI models in response to well-crafted prompts.

Inputs

- **Refined Prompts**: Prepared in the Specification phase, detailing exactly what is to be generated.
- **Model or API Access**: Access to a generative model (e.g., an in-house LLM or a third-party API) along with any necessary tokens or credentials.
- **Data / Code Repositories**: Additional context (e.g., style guidelines, existing code snippets) that the model can reference.

Outputs

- **AI-Generated Artifacts**: This can include entire code modules, test scripts, or user documentation.
- **Feedback Log**: Notes from developers and stakeholders regarding the quality, correctness, or clarity of the generated outputs.

Artifacts

- **Draft Code**: A repository branch or file containing newly generated code.
- **Iterative Prompt History**: Records of each prompt used, enabling teams to refine and reuse effective prompts.

Example

A retail organization fine-tunes an LLM on its internal C# codebase. Developers submit prompts like *"Create a product catalog controller in ASP.NET Core using these established design patterns and data access libraries."* The result is AI-generated code that can be manually reviewed and merged into the broader codebase.

Chapter 9: Transformation

Definition
Transformation involves converting existing artifacts into new formats, languages, or architectures. This may include porting a legacy system from Java to Kotlin or restructuring database schemas based on emerging patterns discovered by AI.

Inputs

- **Existing Artifacts**: Source code or data structures in their current format.
- **Transformation Requirements**: Desired target format or architecture specifications (e.g., microservices).
- **Tooling / Scripts**: Utilities or AI-based modules that assist in code or data transformation.

Outputs

- **Converted Code or Assets**: The same functionality in a new language or framework.
- **Conversion Report**: Documentation highlighting differences, issues, or enhancements uncovered during transformation.

Artifacts

- **Side-by-Side Comparison**: A reference that matches the old artifact to the newly transformed version.
- **Automated Refactoring Logs**: Records of any automated or AI-assisted refactoring steps.

Example

A manufacturing company uses an AI-driven process to **transform** a monolithic Java application into microservices in Spring Boot. The AI model suggests partition boundaries and automatically generates new service endpoints, producing both the microservices and a **Comparison Document** that describes old vs. new service interactions.

Chapter 10: Replacement

Definition
Replacement swaps out outdated or underperforming components with modern AI-generated modules. It's typically performed when existing assets are beyond simple refactoring or are blocking new features.

Inputs

- **Legacy Modules**: Outdated code, libraries, or processes identified for replacement.
- **Replacement Criteria**: Performance targets, compliance considerations, or user experience goals that guide the creation of new assets.
- **Risk Assessment**: Potential impacts on system stability or user workflows when major components change.

Outputs

- **New Modules**: AI-generated or re-written components that meet current technical and functional requirements.
- **Rollback / Contingency Plans**: Prepared strategies if the replacement fails or causes regressions.

Artifacts

- **Retirement Plan**: Document describing how the old module will be decommissioned or archived.
- **Pilot Release Notes**: Summaries for stakeholders, explaining the differences between old and new functionalities.

Example

An insurance firm identifies an aging claims-processing module that no longer meets data privacy rules. The development team runs a generative process to create a new, compliant module and carefully phases out the old code, maintaining a **pilot environment** for direct comparison.

Chapter 11: Integration

Definition
Integration ensures that newly generated artifacts coexist harmoniously with existing systems, databases, and services. It involves bridging generative outputs with established workflows, APIs, or third-party solutions.

Inputs

- **System Architecture**: Documentation of how existing components communicate, including data flows and dependencies.
- **Generated Modules**: Artifacts from Generation, Transformation, or Replacement.
- **Integration Criteria**: Protocol standards, performance metrics, or data format requirements.

Outputs

- **Integrated Systems**: Successfully merged modules, functional within the broader environment.
- **Integration Testing Results**: Records demonstrating that the system operates without regression or instability.

Artifacts

- **API Contracts**: Formal definitions (e.g., OpenAPI specs) specifying communication rules.
- **Integration Test Suites**: Automated scripts verifying new modules work with legacy services.

Example

A global e-commerce platform uses GDF to generate new checkout features. The **Integration** step includes linking these features to existing payment gateways and user authentication flows. Teams produce an **API Contract** that the generative model references to ensure consistent data structures.

Chapter 12: Separation

Definition
Separation involves carving out parts of a monolithic or tightly coupled system into standalone modules or microservices, often aided by AI-driven refactoring or code analysis.

Inputs

- **Monolithic Codebase**: The existing large-scale application requiring decomposition.
- **Service Boundaries**: Identified logical boundaries or domains that can be isolated.
- **Performance Profiles**: Metrics indicating hotspots or bottlenecks, guiding which parts to separate first.

Outputs

- **Independent Services**: Smaller, more maintainable modules, each with clearer boundaries.
- **Updated Architecture Map**: A new system diagram showing each separated service and its interactions.

Artifacts

- **Domain Definition Documents**: Describe each separated domain's responsibilities and data models.
- **Refactoring Logs**: AI-generated suggestions for how to split code effectively.

Example

An HR platform suffering performance issues decides to separate its payroll module from the main system. AI-based refactoring suggestions highlight dependencies, enabling a smooth extraction. After the transformation, there is a distinct **payroll microservice**, with dedicated endpoints and a streamlined codebase.

Chapter 13: Consolidation

Definition
Consolidation merges disparate or redundant modules, microservices, or data sources into a single, more efficient system. AI-assisted analysis can detect overlapping functionality or data duplication.

Inputs

- **Existing Services or Databases**: Multiple systems delivering similar functionality.
- **Consolidation Criteria**: Performance targets, cost optimization goals, or simplified user experiences.
- **Data Mapping**: Schemas or data flow diagrams that highlight overlapping fields or tables.

Outputs

- **Unified Service or Database**: A consolidated system that replaces multiple smaller ones.

- **Retirement / Migration Plans**: Guidance on phasing out old systems or merging data safely.

Artifacts

- **Consolidation Blueprint**: Document describing the plan for merging functionality.
- **Migration Scripts**: AI-generated scripts that unify data while preserving integrity.

Example

A large healthtech enterprise merges three separate patient portals into a single platform. Using an AI-based code and data analysis, teams identify duplicated user authentication flows and unify them into one consolidated service, guided by a **Consolidation Blueprint**.

Chapter 14: Templating

Definition
Templating standardizes common code structures, UI components, or documentation patterns. Teams create reusable "patterns" that can be applied across projects to maintain consistency and speed up development.

Inputs

- **Existing Best Practices**: Well-established coding or UI guidelines.
- **Design Systems or Style Guides**: Formal references that define brand identity or user experience standards.
- **Framework / Language Constraints**: The programming environments in which templates are used (React, Django, etc.).

Outputs

- **Reusable Templates**: Boilerplate code, UI layouts, or user guides.
- **Documentation**: Instructions on how to incorporate templates into new or existing projects.

Artifacts

- **Template Library**: A repository containing standardized code snippets or design patterns.
- **Deployment Checklist**: Ensures that new projects using the template follow required steps (e.g., environment variables, dependencies).

Example

A SaaS provider develops a **Template Library** for microservice creation. It includes Dockerfiles, Kubernetes deployments, and standard security configurations. Product teams rely on these templates to spin up new services in hours instead of weeks.

Chapter 15: Visualization

Definition
Visualization deals with creating clear representations of data, workflows, architectures, or even code relationships. AI can help generate diagrams or dashboards that provide stakeholders with better insights.

Inputs

- **System Metrics / Logs**: Performance data, error rates, user analytics.
- **Architectural Outlines**: High-level diagrams or schematics that need deeper elaboration.
- **User Scenarios**: Specific flows or journeys to visualize (e.g., user login, order processing).

Outputs

- **Diagrams and Dashboards**: Automatically or semi-automatically generated visuals that explain complex systems.
- **Visualization Assets**: Files (e.g., SVG, PNG) or interactive dashboards (e.g., Grafana, Kibana).

Artifacts

- **Visualization Templates**: Standardized chart types or architectural diagrams.
- **Demonstration Decks**: Presentations for leadership or teams highlighting the system's architecture and performance.

Example

In a cloud infrastructure scenario, a DevOps team uses an AI tool to parse Kubernetes cluster logs and auto-generate **node topology diagrams**. This helps them quickly see which clusters are over- or under-utilized.

Chapter 16: Verification

Definition
Verification ensures that AI-generated outputs meet predefined quality standards and truly address the specified requirements. This often includes automated tests, peer reviews, or security audits.

Inputs

- **Acceptance Criteria**: Defined in the Specification knowledge area.
- **Test Data / Test Suites**: Scripts or processes that validate functionality, performance, and resilience.
- **Security and Compliance Guidelines**: Organizational policies to evaluate potential vulnerabilities.

Outputs

- **Validated Artifacts**: Code or documentation that passes all checks and is deemed fit for release.
- **Defect / Issue Logs**: Documented problems identified during verification, along with recommended fixes.

Artifacts

- **Verification Reports**: Summaries of test results and compliance checks.
- **Code Review Notes**: Expert feedback on the quality, maintainability, and security of generated code.

Example

A gaming platform verifying new AI-generated APIs for user matchmaking runs **load tests** to confirm scalability. They produce a **Verification Report** confirming the system can handle peak traffic of one million concurrent users.

Chapter 17: Implementation

Definition
Implementation deals with packaging, deploying, and officially releasing AI-generated functionalities into a live or staging environment. It ensures that the generative outputs are accessible and usable by end-users or downstream systems.

Inputs

- **Deployment Strategy**: Chosen approach (blue-green, canary, or big-bang deployment).
- **Integration Artifacts**: Code or microservices that have completed verification.

- **Infrastructure Specifications**: Details of hosting environments (on-prem, cloud, hybrid).

Outputs

- **Deployed Solutions**: Working code in a production or staging environment.
- **Implementation Records**: Logs tracking version numbers, environment configurations, and deployment times.

Artifacts

- **Release Notes**: Summaries for stakeholders describing new features, known issues, and upgrade steps.
- **Deployment Pipelines**: CI/CD configurations containing AI-generated scripts or tasks.

Example

A telecom provider implements a new recommendation engine for its customers. The **Implementation** step includes using an automated pipeline to deploy each new model version to a staging environment for final checks before going live to all subscribers.

Chapter 18: Optimization

Definition
Optimization focuses on continuous improvement of both AI models and software systems. This includes refining model hyperparameters, tweaking prompts, improving performance, or reducing costs.

Inputs

- **Performance Metrics**: Throughput, latency, CPU/GPU utilization, user satisfaction surveys.

- **Usage Logs**: Logs revealing usage patterns, error rates, or frequent user flows.
- **Feedback from Stakeholders**: Requests or complaints driving targeted enhancements.

Outputs

- **Refined Models / Prompts**: Updated model weights or prompt templates delivering better results.
- **System Improvements**: Code or infrastructure adjustments that boost performance or user experience.

Artifacts

- **Optimization Backlog**: Running list of improvements to be triaged and scheduled.
- **Performance Dashboards**: Graphical representations of improvements over time.

Example

A fintech startup monitors the performance of its generative chat assistant for loan applications. After detecting slow response times during peak hours, the team invests in GPU optimizations and model tuning. They keep an **Optimization Backlog** to track these performance gains.

Chapter 19: Security & Risk Management

Definition
Security & Risk Management ensures that AI-generated outputs, as well as the processes surrounding them, comply with internal and external standards for data protection, access control, and threat mitigation.

Inputs

- **Risk Assessments**: Organizational-level risk registers that highlight possible security or compliance hazards.
- **Security Policies**: Guidelines for encryption, identity and access management, and code vulnerability scanning.
- **AI-Specific Concerns**: Potential model bias, data leakage, or malicious prompt injection.

Outputs

- **Mitigation Plans**: Strategies to address identified risks (e.g., restricted prompts, secure data enclaves).
- **Security Audit Trails**: Logged evidence of reviews and sign-offs demonstrating compliance.

Artifacts

- **Threat Models**: Documents mapping potential attack vectors, particularly around AI-generated code.
- **Incident Response Plans**: Procedures for quickly reacting to security breaches or compliance violations.

Example

A healthcare company requires HIPAA-compliant systems. During generation, the model must avoid exposing protected health information (PHI). **Security & Risk Management** activities include scanning generated code for potential data leaks and ensuring logs do not contain sensitive patient data.

Chapter 20: Generative Pipelines

Definition
Generative Pipelines unify the various tasks—prompt creation, code generation, testing, versioning—into a cohesive flow. By standardizing these steps, teams avoid ad hoc or inconsistent approaches.

Inputs

- **Existing DevOps / CI-CD Practices**: Scripting, automation tools, build and release processes.
- **Model Integration Points**: Where in the pipeline the AI model is invoked, whether for code generation, testing, or documentation creation.
- **Feedback Loops**: Mechanisms (e.g., user input, code reviews) for improving generative steps.

Outputs

- **Automated Generative Flows**: End-to-end pipeline scripts or workflows.
- **Pipeline Documentation**: Clear instructions on how to configure and maintain the generative pipeline.

Artifacts

- **Version-Controlled Prompts**: Source-controlled text prompts or JSON configurations describing generation tasks.
- **Build/Deployment Scripts**: Code that orchestrates how AI outputs are compiled, tested, and deployed.

Example

An automotive software team sets up a Jenkins pipeline that automatically calls a text-to-code LLM. Whenever a developer merges changes, the pipeline regenerates certain unit tests based on the updated code, then runs the entire test suite. This helps keep tests in sync with minimal manual intervention.

Chapter 21: Compliance & Governance

Definition
Compliance & Governance centers on aligning generative AI

initiatives with legal, regulatory, and organizational policies. It also includes governance structures that define accountability, approvals, and escalation paths.

Inputs

- **Regulatory Requirements**: Industry-specific rules (e.g., GDPR for data privacy, FDA guidelines for healthcare software).
- **Organizational Policies**: Internal guidelines on data usage, intellectual property, and brand consistency.
- **Governance Framework**: Decision-making structures that define roles and escalation channels.

Outputs

- **Compliance Checklists**: Documented evidence that generative artifacts meet necessary legal and corporate guidelines.
- **Governance Reports**: Periodic summaries of generative AI activities, highlighting compliance status and areas needing attention.

Artifacts

- **Audit Trails**: Detailed logs showing who prompted the AI, when, and what was generated.
- **Policy Repository**: Updated guidelines for generative AI usage, version-controlled for accountability.

Example

A pharmaceutical company's **Compliance & Governance** process enforces strict workflows for generating and documenting software supporting clinical trials. Each AI-generated artifact is automatically tagged and reviewed by a governance board to ensure adherence to regulatory protocols.

Chapter 22: Collaboration & Communication

Definition
Collaboration & Communication ensures all stakeholders—technical, business, compliance, and end-users—are informed and engaged throughout the generative development process. Clear communication channels foster cooperation and mitigate resistance to change.

Inputs

- **Stakeholder Roster**: List of teams and individuals impacted or involved.
- **Engagement Plans**: Defined strategies on how and when to communicate updates, gather feedback, or escalate issues.
- **Feedback Tools**: Mechanisms like Slack channels, survey forms, or stakeholder review sessions.

Outputs

- **Engaged Stakeholders**: A community of users, managers, and leaders who understand generative AI goals and processes.
- **Communication Records**: Meeting minutes, email threads, or dashboards reflecting key decisions and updates.

Artifacts

- **Collaboration Platforms**: Shared repositories, wikis, or chat tools that centralize information.
- **Announcement Templates**: Pre-defined structures for delivering project updates or newly generated artifacts.

Example

A global e-commerce company invests in frequent demo sessions where newly generated modules are showcased. Product managers,

QA leads, and compliance officers provide immediate feedback, fostering a culture of **transparent collaboration** and quick iteration.

Chapter 23: Scaling & Sustaining

Definition
Scaling & Sustaining focuses on expanding successful generative initiatives across multiple teams or business units, as well as ensuring long-term viability in terms of maintenance, upgrades, and continuous improvement.

Inputs

- **Pilot Success Metrics**: Results from initial generative projects that serve as proof of concept.
- **Enterprise Roadmaps**: Long-term plans indicating where generative AI can be replicated or further expanded.
- **Resource Availability**: Budget, skill sets, and infrastructure capacity to sustain growth.

Outputs

- **Scaled Generative Programs**: Multiple teams adopting and benefiting from GDF-based workflows.
- **Long-Term Maintenance Plans**: Provisions for regular model updates, hardware refreshes, or staff training.

Artifacts

- **Playbooks**: Step-by-step guides for new teams looking to adopt GDF quickly.
- **Center of Excellence (CoE) Charters**: Formal structures that oversee best practices, training, and governance for generative AI across the enterprise.

Example

A multinational bank that initially introduced generative AI for internal chatbots extends the approach to automated code generation for multiple divisions. They create a **Center of Excellence** that maintains standardized prompts, organizes training for new dev teams, and monitors enterprise-wide generative AI adoption metrics.

Chapter 24: Competency (New Knowledge Area)

Definition
Competency addresses the human element of generative development. It examines the **skill and experience** levels needed to effectively leverage AI in building software. A competent generative development engineer knows how to interpret, validate, and refine AI outputs, ensuring that software remains maintainable, secure, and aligned with best practices.

Inputs

- **Skill Assessments**: Evaluations of engineers' understanding of both the domain and the technology stack.
- **Training Programs**: Curricula that cover prompt engineering, AI model usage, debugging, and domain-specific standards.
- **Mentorship / Onboarding Plans**: Structured approaches to guide new or less experienced developers in effectively collaborating with AI.

Outputs

- **Validated Competency Levels**: A clear map of which engineers are ready for advanced generative tasks, and who needs further training.
- **Sustainable Expertise**: A workforce capable of long-term AI integration, ensuring quality, security, and maintainability.

Artifacts

- **Skill Matrix**: A document or tool that classifies required generative AI skills, from beginner to expert.
- **Learning Pathways**: Recommended courses, workshops, or labs, possibly culminating in certification or internal accreditation.

Example: Experienced vs. Inexperienced Developer

- **Scenario**: Both developers are tasked with generating a new microservice using an AI model.
    - **Experienced Generative Engineer**: Crafts precise prompts, references corporate coding standards, and conducts thorough peer reviews. The resulting code adheres to best practices, is secure, and easy to maintain.
    - **Inexperienced or No-Experience Person**: Uses generic prompts, overlooks error handling, and fails to validate code thoroughly. The resulting microservice is initially functional but contains hidden security flaws and lacks proper documentation, leading to issues in production.

By emphasizing **Competency**, organizations ensure that generative AI is wielded effectively rather than becoming a shortcut that could compromise quality or compliance.

PART III: IMPLEMENTATION GUIDANCE

This section synthesizes the GDF Knowledge Areas into a **step-by-step** implementation roadmap. It also addresses **organizational readiness**, **pilot strategies**, **scaling approaches**, and **ongoing maintenance**—all grounded in the core principle that successful generative AI initiatives require alignment between people, processes, and technology.

Chapter 25: GDF Implementation Roadmap

25.1 Overview of the Roadmap

The GDF Implementation Roadmap provides a **holistic** path from initial strategic planning to widespread enterprise adoption. While each organization will tailor the sequence and emphasis based on its context, the roadmap typically unfolds across four main stages:

1. **Stage 1: Readiness and Initial Alignment**
2. **Stage 2: Pilot Execution and Validation**
3. **Stage 3: Scaling and Standardization**
4. **Stage 4: Continuous Improvement and Sustained Adoption**

Within these stages, organizations leverage the **19 GDF Knowledge Areas** to build robust generative development capabilities.

25.2 Integrating Knowledge Areas into the Roadmap

Roadmap Stage	Relevant GDF Knowledge Areas
Stage 1: Readiness & Alignment	Ideation, Competency, Collaboration & Communication, Security & Risk Management, Compliance & Governance
Stage 2: Pilot & Validation	Specification, Generation, Verification, Implementation, Competency, Collaboration & Communication
Stage 3: Scaling & Standardization	Integration, Separation, Consolidation, Templating, Generative Pipelines, Scaling & Sustaining
Stage 4: Continuous Improvement	Optimization, Transformation, Replacement, Competency, Compliance & Governance, Security & Risk Management, Sustainment

The table above suggests typical "focal points" for each stage; in practice, many Knowledge Areas run in parallel or repeat based on the project's nature.

Chapter 26: Organizational Maturity & Readiness

26.1 Assessing Current Maturity Levels

Before launching a generative AI program, organizations often conduct a **readiness assessment** to gauge both technical infrastructure and cultural acceptance. This step aligns strongly with the **Ideation** and **Competency** Knowledge Areas, ensuring teams have:

- **Technical Infrastructure**: Availability of GPU/TPU resources, robust CI/CD pipelines, and data governance.
- **Skills & Competency**: Engineers, QA specialists, and product owners who understand AI basics and domain complexities.
- **Change Appetite**: A culture open to adopting new technologies and methods, with leadership support.

Common maturity assessments include scoring models (e.g., on a 1–5 scale) across domains such as **Data Preparedness**, **AI Literacy**, **Security Posture**, **Leadership Buy-In**, and **Existing Automation Practices**.

26.2 Building the Core Team

Based on readiness results, organizations often form a **cross-functional core team** for GDF adoption. This team typically includes:

- **Generative AI Engineer / Lead**: Oversees prompt engineering, model integration, and technical frameworks.
- **Product/Project Lead**: Manages scope, user stories, and ensures generative outputs align with stakeholder needs.
- **Compliance & Security Rep**: Reviews data handling, code security, and compliance frameworks.
- **DevOps / Infrastructure Engineer**: Sets up pipelines for continuous integration of AI-generated artifacts.
- **Competency Advisor** (could be a senior engineer or solutions architect): Monitors the skill development of junior staff to ensure quality outputs.

26.3 Addressing Gaps and Risks

If the assessment uncovers significant skill or infrastructure gaps, the organization can:

1. **Invest in Training**: Workshops on prompt engineering, code quality, security, or domain-specific AI use.
2. **Pilot with External Partners**: Work with AI consultancies or platform vendors to accelerate learning.
3. **Acquire Tools and Platforms**: Adopt managed services for model hosting, data pipelines, or security scanning.

Articulating these needs clearly in a **Readiness Report** ensures leadership and financial stakeholders see the required investments and timelines.

Chapter 27: Stage 1 – Readiness & Initial Alignment

27.1 Set the Vision and Scope

Start by defining the **purpose of generative AI** within the organization. This might be:

- **Improving Developer Productivity**: Automating boilerplate coding tasks.
- **Enhancing Product Features**: Embedding AI-driven functionality (e.g., chatbots or recommendation engines).
- **Streamlining Compliance**: Using AI to generate or validate compliance documentation.

Key artifacts here include a **Generative AI Charter** or a **Vision Statement** that outlines high-level goals and success metrics.

27.2 Ideation Workshops

Run structured **Ideation** sessions to generate use cases. Involve domain experts, experienced developers, product managers, and compliance officers to ensure broad coverage. Examples of topics:

- **Which manual tasks eat most of our development time?**
- **Can we unify UI frameworks via AI-driven Templating?**
- **Do we have repetitive or simple code patterns ripe for AI generation?**

Outputs of these sessions feed into a **Prioritized Idea List**.

27.3 Ensuring Competency

Use a **Skill Matrix** (from the Competency Knowledge Area) to categorize employees:

- **AI Novices**: Need foundational training on LLM usage and basic prompt engineering.
- **Intermediate**: Comfortable with some AI usage but require deeper domain expertise.
- **Advanced**: Potential mentors or advisors who can shape best practices.

Plan onboarding or training modules accordingly. The difference between **experienced** vs. **inexperienced** generative engineers can drastically alter project success, maintainability, and security. Ensure that initial use cases pair seasoned engineers with novices for real-time mentorship.

27.4 Aligning Security & Governance

Perform an initial **Security & Risk Management** review, focusing on:

- **Data Sensitivity**: Identifying whether personal or financial data might be exposed.
- **Access Controls**: Ensuring only authorized teams can invoke generative models or access prompts.

- **Regulatory Constraints**: Outlining necessary governance or compliance sign-offs, especially in regulated industries (finance, healthcare, etc.).

Create or refine a **Generative AI Risk Register** capturing possible threats (e.g., prompt injection, code vulnerabilities, IP infringement) and suggested mitigation steps.

Chapter 28: Stage 2 – Pilot Execution and Validation

28.1 Selecting a Pilot Project

Choose an initial project with **clear success criteria** and **manageable complexity**. This pilot should allow teams to learn but not be so critical that failure jeopardizes entire business lines. Examples:

- **Automated Test Generation** for a mid-size module.
- **Code Generation** for an internal utility library.
- **Documentation Generation** for existing APIs.

28.2 Defining Specifications and Prompts

Within the pilot, emphasize **Specification** to ensure clarity:

- Write **Prompt Templates** that detail coding style, error handling, logging, and performance constraints.
- Outline acceptance criteria in a **Generative Requirement** document.

For instance, a specification might read:

"Generate a Python-based microservice that handles up to 5,000 concurrent connections, logs requests to a centralized system, uses OAuth2, and must pass our existing integration tests for user authentication."

28.3 Running the Generation Phase

During the pilot, the **Generation** knowledge area comes to life:

1. **Prompt Submission**: The generative AI engineer provides the model with context (existing codebase references, relevant libraries).
2. **Review & Iteration**: Senior engineers validate outputs, providing feedback to refine prompts.
3. **Version Control**: Each AI-generated artifact is checked into a separate branch for peer review.

Artifacts generated might include initial code modules, partial documentation, or test scripts. Maintain a **Prompt History** to track which instructions yielded the best outcomes.

28.4 Validating and Integrating Outputs

Once the pilot solution reaches a functional milestone:

- **Verification**: Conduct automated tests, security scans, and peer code reviews.
- **Integration**: Merge the validated code into the main repository. If the pilot is a standalone feature, deploy to a staging environment.

Collect metrics (e.g., time saved, lines of code auto-generated, number of defects found) to measure pilot success. Summarize these findings in a **Pilot Review Report**.

28.5 Building Competency Through the Pilot

Use the pilot as a **real-world training ground**:

- Pair novices with advanced AI-savvy engineers.
- Document **lessons learned** on prompt design, AI model quirks, and code acceptance thresholds.
- Evaluate each participant's skills after the pilot; update the **Skill Matrix** to reflect new competencies.

This ensures the knowledge gained is retained and fosters a pipeline of skilled professionals who can lead future generative AI projects.

Chapter 29: Stage 3 – Scaling & Standardization

After a successful pilot demonstrates the viability of generative AI in one or more areas, the next step is **scaling** these practices to other teams and **standardizing** processes to maintain consistency across the organization.

29.1 Laying the Foundation for Scale

1. **Establish a Center of Excellence (CoE)**
   - **Definition**: A dedicated group tasked with curating best practices, providing training, and overseeing the expansion of generative AI capabilities.
   - **Responsibilities**:
     - **Template Creation**: Develop standardized code, prompt, and policy templates.
     - **Community Building**: Host internal hackathons or "brown bag" sessions to share knowledge and success stories.
     - **Tool Management**: Evaluate and recommend AI platforms, model hosting services, or third-party integrations.
2. **Develop an Onboarding Framework**
   - **Purpose**: Streamline the induction of new teams into the Generative Development Framework (GDF).
   - **Components**:
     - **Training Modules**: Core AI fundamentals, prompt engineering, domain best practices.
     - **Role Definitions**: Clear outlines of what a "Generative AI Engineer," "Compliance Lead," or "DevOps Integrator" does in the context of GDF.

- **Early Mentorship**: For each new team, assign a "buddy" from the CoE or a more experienced team.
3. **Assess Cultural Readiness**
   - **Checkpoints**:
     - **Leadership Buy-In**: Ensure new department heads are on board.
     - **Developer Attitudes**: Gauge openness to adopting or refining generative methods.
   - **Mitigation**: If any hesitancy is discovered, schedule interactive demos or run small-scale proofs-of-concept to highlight the benefits.

29.2 Standardizing Processes and Artifacts

1. **Common Prompt Libraries**
   - **Description**: A repository containing well-tested prompts for recurring development tasks (e.g., unit test generation, CRUD APIs, UI templates).
   - **Benefits**:
     - **Consistency**: Uniform code style and security measures across different teams.
     - **Efficiency**: Reduced setup time for new teams or projects.
2. **Unified Security and Compliance Checks**
   - **Why It Matters**: Different teams may inadvertently create policy gaps. A single, well-defined set of checks fosters a safer environment.
   - **Methods**:
     - **Automated Scanning**: Integrate scanning tools (static analysis, vulnerability detection) into generative pipelines.
     - **Compliance Templates**: Predefined policy checklists to ensure data, code, and user interfaces meet regulatory needs.
3. **Template-Driven Integration**

- o **Focus**: GDF Knowledge Areas like **Templating, Integration**, and **Generative Pipelines** converge here.
- o **Outcome**: Standard pipelines that define exactly how generative outputs move from creation, through testing, into deployment.

29.3 Organizational Communication and Stakeholder Engagement

1. **Periodic Town Halls**
   - o **Purpose**: Keep the wider organization informed of new successes, lessons learned, and updates to GDF best practices.
   - o **Frequency**: Quarterly or monthly, depending on the pace of adoption.
2. **Scaling Knowledge Sharing**
   - o **Internal Platforms**: Confluence pages, Slack channels, or wikis dedicated to GDF discussions.
   - o **Expert Panels**: Encourage employees recognized as advanced users (or "Generative Champions") to field questions and mentor peers.
3. **Feedback Loops**
   - o **Mechanism**: Collect input via retrospectives, surveys, or iterative design sessions.
   - o **Application**: Feed the insights back into the CoE to refine training materials, templates, and recommended best practices.

29.4 Example: Multi-Region Rollout

- **Scenario**: An automotive manufacturer that piloted AI-assisted documentation generation now wants each regional R&D center to adopt GDF for code generation, testing, and compliance.
- **Actions**:

- Central CoE in the headquarters develops standardized **Prompt Libraries** for common tasks in automotive software (e.g., sensor data processing).
- Regional leads undergo onboarding sessions, after which they refine prompts for local languages or regulatory nuances.
- **Result:** In six months, all R&D centers report a consistent code style, faster onboarding of new engineers, and reduced rework due to standardized generative pipelines.

Chapter 30: Stage 4 – Continuous Improvement & Sustained Adoption

Once generative development is standardized, the organization shifts focus to **long-term sustainability** and **continuous enhancement** of GDF practices.

30.1 Ongoing Model and Prompt Optimization

1. **Data Refresh Cycles**
   - **Rationale:** As codebases and business requirements evolve, the underlying AI models must reflect current patterns and best practices.
   - **Approach:**
     - **Scheduled Retraining:** Periodically fine-tune or retrain models with updated code repositories or domain knowledge.
     - **Monitoring:** Track potential performance declines (model drift), prompting re-checks of accuracy, security, and compliance.
2. **Prompt Evolution**
   - **Incremental Refinement:** Keep logs of successful vs. less effective prompts, systematically updating your **Prompt Libraries**.

- Team Insights: Encourage engineers to record new or improved prompts in a shared repository, describing the context and outcomes.
3. **Performance Dashboards**
   - **Focus**: GDF Knowledge Area **Optimization**.
   - **Key Metrics**: Execution time for generation, code defect rates, number of merge conflicts resolved, average developer satisfaction scores.

30.2 Handling Major Technology Shifts

1. **New Language or Framework Adoption**
   - **Challenge**: Integrating a new framework (e.g., a next-generation front-end library) with existing generative processes.
   - **Solution**: Create new templates, prompt guidelines, and model training materials for the new ecosystem. Update the **Separation**, **Transformation**, or **Replacement** Knowledge Areas as needed.
2. **Tooling Upgrades**
   - **Scenario**: Third-party AI platforms release new features or improved models.
   - **Recommended Steps**:
     - **Pilot** the new tools on a low-risk module before broad adoption.
     - **Document** changes in your generative pipeline or coding standards.
     - **Train** teams to ensure they leverage new capabilities effectively.
3. **Revisiting Governance and Security**
   - **Reason**: As technologies evolve, so do security concerns (e.g., new forms of prompt injection, compliance updates).
   - **Action**: Update **Security & Risk Management** protocols, refine compliance checklists, and re-train staff.

30.3 Sustaining a Generative AI Culture

1. **Reward Systems**
   - **Purpose**: Recognize individuals or teams that significantly advance GDF adoption or create novel solutions.
   - **Methods**: Internal awards, promotions, or acknowledgment in company newsletters.
2. **Innovation Programs**
   - **Hackathons**: Encourage employees to explore unconventional uses of generative AI, from creative code solutions to advanced analytics.
   - **Knowledge Exchanges**: Routine meetups where teams demonstrate how they overcame specific challenges in generative development.
3. **Competency Refresh**
   - **Reason**: Technology moves quickly, and new hires join with varying skill levels.
   - **Implementation**: Revisit the **Competency** Knowledge Area, updating learning pathways and mentorship initiatives. Maintain a dynamic **Skill Matrix** that evolves with both personnel changes and technology updates.

Chapter 31: Consolidating Best Practices and Artifacts

31.1 Comprehensive Artifact Library

At this stage, the organization typically has a robust **Artifact Library** that covers:

- **Prompt Templates** for code generation, test creation, and documentation.
- **Deployment Checklists** that detail necessary steps for rolling AI-generated code into production.

- **Model Retraining Schedules** or guidelines ensuring continuous alignment with evolving code standards.
- **Security & Compliance Scripts** integrated into the pipeline, scanning for vulnerabilities or policy violations.

Benefits:

- **Repeatability**: Teams can replicate successful approaches in new domains or product lines.
- **Resilience**: By formalizing proven methods, the organization is less reliant on individual knowledge and can maintain stability through staff transitions.

31.2 Templates and Guides

Some recommended templates and guides include:

1. **GDF Onboarding Guide**
   - **Contents**: Overview of Knowledge Areas, recommended training resources, and a quick-start checklist for new hires or new teams.
2. **Generative Pipeline Configuration Template**
   - **Purpose**: Offers a standard way to set up or modify CI/CD pipelines that incorporate AI generation tasks.
   - **Key Sections**: Version control integration, environment variables for model endpoints, triggers for code or test generation, security scanning steps.
3. **Competency Skill Matrix**
   - **Definition**: Maps out skill requirements for each role, from "Basic Prompt Crafting" to "Advanced AI Pipeline Development."
   - **Usage**: Managers can quickly assess training needs, build balanced teams, or guide career development discussions.
4. **Risk and Security Checklist**

- o **Details**: Standard steps for verifying compliance, including data anonymization, usage logs, encryption standards, and third-party library checks.
- o **Maintenance**: Regularly updated to reflect new threats or regulatory changes.

31.3 Case Studies for Reference

Maintaining a **Case Study Repository** of successful (and even unsuccessful) GDF projects fosters shared learning. Each case can detail:

- **Business Problem**: Why generative AI was chosen.
- **Solution Approach**: Which Knowledge Areas were most critical, how prompts were designed, key pipeline steps.
- **Outcomes**: Efficiency improvements, code quality metrics, developer satisfaction.
- **Lessons Learned**: Prompt mistakes, overlooked compliance issues, or misaligned expectations.

Over time, this repository becomes an invaluable internal resource, helping new teams avoid pitfalls and accelerate adoption.

PART IV: PRACTICAL TOOLS & REFERENCE MATERIALS

In this section, we focus on the **key artifacts, templates, and best practices** that help organizations implement GDF in a consistent and scalable way. Instead of providing raw code examples, we concentrate on **processes, cultural shifts, and metrics** that guide teams to leverage generative AI effectively. The goal is to ensure that a skilled software developer (for instance, a Node.js specialist) can expand their capabilities across multiple domains—front-end frameworks, new programming languages, or advanced security practices—by relying on generative AI for support.

Chapter 32: Sample Templates and Checklists

32.1 Project Initiation & Readiness Template

Purpose
A simple template to ensure that each generative AI effort starts with clarity around objectives, scope, responsibilities, and readiness. It helps confirm that leadership, technical teams, and compliance officers share the same vision and priorities.

1. **Project Overview**
    o   Project name, sponsoring department, and key stakeholders.
2. **Business Objectives**
    o   Desired outcomes: improved quality, reduced development time, additional platform coverage, etc.
3. **Generative AI Use Case**
    o   Specific areas where AI will assist: code generation, test automation, design prototyping, etc.
4. **Readiness Factors**
    o   Skill availability, infrastructure capacity, alignment with corporate strategy.
5. **Risks and Constraints**
    o   Known bottlenecks or data/privacy concerns, resource or time limitations.
6. **Next Steps**
    o   Immediate tasks for finalizing the pilot or moving toward production.

Key Outcomes

- Ensures alignment among all parties from the start.
- Identifies necessary approvals (budget, security clearance, etc.).
- Highlights skill gaps to address before diving into generative AI projects.

32.2 Generative Requirements & Prompt Specification Template

Purpose
This template helps structure how teams define **what** they expect from the AI and **how** they will measure success. It might include prompt guidelines, acceptance criteria, and references to relevant design patterns or security rules.

1. **Feature / Module Summary**
   - High-level description of the software component or domain area.
2. **Functional Goals**
   - Specific capabilities or tasks the AI-generated output must fulfill (e.g., handling authentication, logging, performance constraints).
3. **Constraints & Standards**
   - Coding conventions, security rules, required frameworks or libraries.
4. **Prompt Details**
   - Base prompt, context, and any domain examples the AI should reference.
5. **Validation Criteria**
   - Automated checks, peer reviews, or benchmark tests that define "acceptance."
6. **Revision History & Lessons Learned**
   - Tracking how prompts evolve over time, capturing best practices.

Key Outcomes

- Reduces ambiguity for development teams.
- Establishes consistent, repeatable patterns for prompt creation, ensuring reusability across projects.
- Documents lessons learned, accelerating future generative tasks.

32.3 Compliance & Governance Checklist

Purpose
Ensures the generated artifacts meet **organizational policies** and **regulatory requirements**. This checklist can be integrated into an automated pipeline or reviewed manually at major milestones.

1. **Data Protection**
   - Confidential or personal data handling, anonymization, and encryption checks.
2. **Intellectual Property**
   - Verifying the use of open-source or third-party libraries and their respective licenses.
3. **Security Controls**
   - Confirming no sensitive credentials appear in generated outputs, ensuring vulnerability scans are up to date.
4. **Documentation & Audit Trails**
   - Keeping records of AI usage (which prompts, who approved them, model version), and storing sign-off logs.
5. **Responsible Use**
   - Verifying that outputs do not inadvertently create harmful or misleading functionality, if applicable.

Key Outcomes

- Reduces security risks by catching potential vulnerabilities early.
- Simplifies audits and proofs of compliance.
- Fosters trust among stakeholders, demonstrating that generative AI usage is well-governed.

Chapter 33: Practical Implementation Scenarios

While the GDF is universally adaptable, the following scenarios illustrate **how processes, culture, and metrics** can transform an organization's software engineering approach.

33.1 Multi-Language AI Environment

Scenario
A large enterprise with teams in different technology stacks (e.g., Node.js, Java, Python) wants to **centralize** generative AI support to boost efficiency and code quality across the board.

Key Considerations

- **Central Registry of Model Use**: Maintain a knowledge base outlining each team's domain (backend, frontend, data processing) and the generative AI prompts or patterns that best suit them.
- **Cultural Shift**: Encourage Node.js experts to apply generative prompts for front-end frameworks (React, Angular) without fear of "stepping out of their lane." This fosters cross-domain collaboration and skill development.
- **Metrics**: Track how many multi-language tasks are completed through AI assistance vs. purely manual coding. Evaluate code quality improvements via peer reviews and defect rates.

Success Indicators

- Reduced "time-to-first-commit" for developers branching into new languages or frameworks.
- Consistent code standards across languages, indicating the AI is applying enterprise-wide guidelines effectively.

33.2 Advanced Security & Risk Management

Scenario
A financial institution must adhere to stringent data protection and security protocols while accelerating development with generative AI.

Key Considerations

- **Secure Workflows**: Only authorized personnel can feed prompts or train/fine-tune the AI model. All data is anonymized or masked.
- **Automated Checkpoints**: At each milestone (e.g., dev, QA, production), a security checklist is triggered to confirm no sensitive data is revealed or used incorrectly.
- **Metrics**: Log the number and severity of security incidents or near misses. Correlate these with improvements in generative prompt guidelines.

Success Indicators

- Zero security breaches directly attributed to AI-generated artifacts.
- Reduced manual security overhead, thanks to integrated compliance and governance steps.

33.3 Organization-Wide Scaling

Scenario
After a pilot in one department, an enterprise wants to scale generative AI adoption to other lines of business, ensuring consistent processes, templates, and success metrics.

Key Considerations

- **Center of Excellence (CoE)**: A specialized team to train new adopters, maintain best practices, and track enterprise-wide usage.
- **Common Onboarding Kits**: Standardized prompts, templates, and checklists for each domain or technology stack.
- **Metrics**: Use leaderboards or dashboards that measure improved productivity (e.g., lines of code generated, time saved), code quality, and cross-team collaboration.

Success Indicators

- Multiple departments using GDF artifacts consistently.
- Creation of a recognized "Generative AI Community" inside the company, where engineers share experiences and best practices.

Chapter 34: Advanced Topics and Future Considerations

34.1 Handling Model Drift Without Direct Code Snippets

Context
Over time, AI models may produce outputs that drift from established coding standards or best practices. This can be due to changes in the codebase, newly introduced libraries, or model updates.

Strategies

1. **Quality Benchmarks**: Continuously measure code complexity, maintainability, and security posture.
2. **Scheduled Model Reviews**: Conduct monthly or quarterly reviews where advanced users and architects assess generative outputs against the organization's evolving needs.
3. **Prompt Refinement**: Update existing prompt templates to reflect new best practices or discourage outdated patterns.

34.2 Effective Maintenance Without Direct Code Snippets

1. **Retrospective Analysis**: Periodically examine projects that heavily used generative AI to identify successes and failures. Document findings in a central knowledge base.
2. **Feedback Aggregation**: Gather developer and QA insights on where the AI excels or struggles. Use these insights to refine generation guidelines and acceptance criteria.

3. **Lifecycle Management**: If a model becomes outdated or less performant, develop a structured approach for gracefully retiring or archiving it, ensuring minimal disruption to active teams.

Chapter 35: Creating and Measuring a Generative AI Culture

As generative AI matures within an organization, success increasingly depends on **culture**—the collective mindset that guides how teams approach new technologies, continuous learning, and cross-domain collaboration.

1. **Leadership Engagement**
   - **Frequent Showcases**: Leadership celebrates success stories where generative AI significantly accelerated or improved software delivery.
   - **Resource Allocation**: Managers ensure that teams have time and budget for experimentation and skill development.
2. **Metrics That Matter**
   - **Adoption Rate**: Percentage of teams actively utilizing generative AI tools or templates.
   - **Quality Score**: Aggregate measure of issues found in AI-generated code vs. manually written code, indicating the effectiveness of generative standards.
   - **Time-to-Competence**: How quickly a developer can learn a new language or framework using generative AI assistance.
3. **Encouraging Experimentation**
   - **Pilot Grants**: Offer small seed investments for innovative AI-driven ideas.
   - **Internal Marketing**: Create a sense of excitement, framing generative AI as an enabler of personal growth and skill expansion.

PART V: CONCLUSION AND FUTURE DIRECTIONS

In this final section, we bring together the key threads of the Generative Development Framework (GDF), emphasizing **critical success factors**, **organizational considerations**, and **ongoing evolutions** in the field of generative AI. The goal is to provide a clear roadmap for long-term, sustainable adoption—so that organizations can continuously harness generative AI for competitive advantage while maintaining high standards of quality, security, and cross-functional collaboration.

Chapter 36: Core Principles Recap

1. **Phased Lifecycle**
    - **Strategy & Preparation**: Align generative AI initiatives with strategic needs and assess readiness.
    - **Scoping & Planning**: Define scope, success criteria, risk management approaches, and stakeholder engagement.
    - **Generation & Validation**: Use well-structured prompts and rigorous verification processes to ensure high-quality outputs.
    - **Implementation & Monitoring**: Deploy AI-driven software into real-world environments, tracking performance and security.
    - **Sustainment & Evolution**: Continuously refine processes, retrain models, and seek out new opportunities across the organization.
2. **Knowledge Areas**
    The **19** Knowledge Areas of GDF span a holistic range of practices—from **Ideation** and **Specification** to **Verification**, **Compliance & Governance**, and the newly added **Competency** domain. Each area contributes to a structured, repeatable way of incorporating generative AI into software engineering.

3. **Iterative and Adaptive Mindset**
   GDF encourages frequent feedback loops to adjust prompts, refine model training, and incorporate lessons learned. This ensures that AI-driven development efforts remain **agile** in the face of shifting organizational needs or technological evolution.

Chapter 37: Critical Success Factors

37.1 Executive Sponsorship and Leadership Engagement

- **Visible Support**: Leaders who openly champion generative AI can help secure budget, remove organizational barriers, and motivate teams.
- **Clear Alignment**: Tie each generative AI project to tangible business goals—such as reducing time-to-market, scaling to new tech stacks, or improving code quality metrics.

37.2 Competency Development

- **Skill-Building**: The **Competency** Knowledge Area highlights that human expertise remains pivotal. Ensure developers, QA professionals, and product managers are trained to collaborate effectively with generative tools.
- **Mentoring and Cross-Pollination**: Encourage experienced engineers to guide newcomers, share best practices, and build a broader culture of continuous learning.

37.3 Rigorous Security and Compliance

- **Structured Checklists**: Incorporate a compliance and security review at each major project milestone.
- **Integrated Governance**: Governance is not an afterthought; it's woven into every phase, from initial feasibility to final deployment.

37.4 Culture of Collaboration and Communication

- **Transparent Processes**: Regular demos, open forum discussions, and easy-access wikis or chat channels foster knowledge-sharing.
- **Iterative Feedback**: Solicit continuous input from both technical and non-technical stakeholders, refining AI outputs to meet evolving requirements.

37.5 Continuous Improvement Framework

- **Measurement**: Track metrics like defect rates in AI-generated code, prompt success rates, developer satisfaction, and time saved.
- **Model Drift Detection**: Schedule ongoing reviews to ensure the AI model's outputs remain aligned with new coding standards, dependencies, and domain insights.

Chapter 38: Common Pitfalls and How to Avoid Them

1. **Over-Reliance on Automation**
   - **Risk**: Blindly trusting AI outputs without proper human oversight can lead to security loopholes and quality issues.
   - **Mitigation**: Incorporate robust **Verification** practices and encourage human review at all critical junctures.
2. **Insufficient Training or Onboarding**
   - **Risk**: Developers who lack fundamental domain knowledge or prompt engineering skills may produce suboptimal outputs or misuse AI capabilities.
   - **Mitigation**: Establish well-defined onboarding programs and skill matrices to ensure each generative AI initiative is guided by appropriately trained personnel.
3. **Neglecting Documentation**
   - **Risk**: Rapidly generated code, tests, or designs without proper documentation cause confusion and maintainability problems.

- Mitigation: Implement **Templating** and **Documentation** standards, requiring that each artifact includes inline or external documentation.
4. **Data Privacy Oversights**
   - **Risk**: Feeding sensitive information into generative AI models can result in unauthorized data exposure.
   - **Mitigation**: Implement stringent **Security & Compliance** protocols, requiring all data inputs be masked or anonymized when possible.

Chapter 39: Future Trends and Evolving Practices

39.1 Emergence of Specialized Models

- **Domain-Specific AI**: As generative AI matures, we will likely see more **specialized** language models fine-tuned for specific frameworks (e.g., Node.js front-end, .NET microservices, data analytics in R).
- **Continuous Learning Pipelines**: AI models that adapt in near real-time to codebase changes and new best practices may become the norm.

39.2 Enhanced Collaboration Mechanisms

- **Real-Time Prompt Sharing**: A growing number of integrated development environments (IDEs) offer live collaboration features, enabling multiple team members to co-create prompts and see AI-generated suggestions in real time.
- **AI Pair Programming**: Some organizations already treat AI as a "virtual partner," conducting pair programming sessions to improve code quality and reduce ramp-up time on unfamiliar tech stacks.

39.3 Regulatory Evolutions and Societal Factors

- **Growing Compliance Landscape**: Expect stricter regulations around AI usage, data privacy, and potential model biases.

GDF's **Compliance & Governance** area will need to adapt continuously to meet these evolving legal and ethical demands.
- **Public Perception and Trust**: As generative AI becomes more visible in consumer-facing software, maintaining user trust through transparency and responsible usage will be paramount.

39.4 Expanding Roles and Skill Sets

- **Generative AI Specialist**: A new role may emerge, combining software engineering expertise with strong knowledge of AI model internals and prompt design.
- **Hybrid Teams**: Cross-functional groups that blend front-end, back-end, security, DevOps, and data science, all facilitated by AI tools to expedite transitions and knowledge sharing.

Chapter 40: Concluding Thoughts and Final Recommendations

The Generative Development Framework (GDF) offers a **unified, systematic approach** for leveraging generative AI across software development lifecycles. By implementing the framework's phases, knowledge areas, and practical tools:

1. **Organizations Gain Efficiency**: Teams can automate repetitive tasks, accelerate multi-platform initiatives, and spend more time on creativity and innovation.
2. **Developers Enhance Competency**: Skilled engineers evolve into multi-stack specialists, supported by AI to bridge gaps in domain knowledge or language expertise.
3. **Quality and Security Improve**: Rigorous Verification, Security & Risk Management, and Compliance & Governance ensure outputs align with corporate and legal standards.
4. **Sustainable Adoption Ensues**: By following iterative, transparent processes, generative AI becomes embedded in

the organizational culture, enabling long-term success and adaptability.

Ultimately, **success with generative AI** hinges on the synergy between **skilled human oversight, well-defined processes,** and **robust cultural acceptance.** GDF provides the blueprint for navigating this new frontier—one where software engineering and AI converge to deliver solutions faster, smarter, and more securely than ever before.